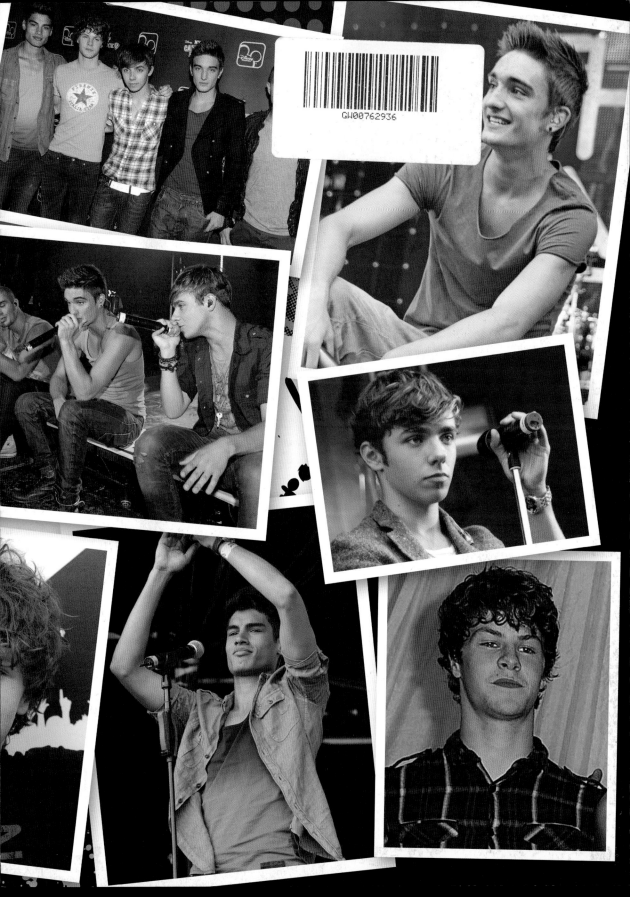

100% The Wanted: The Unofficial Guide
A BANTAM BOOK 978 0 857 51036 5

First published in Great Britain by Bantam,
an imprint of Random House Children's Books
A Random House Group Company

Bantam edition published 2010

1 3 5 7 9 10 8 6 4 2

Text copyright © Bantam Books, 2010

Design by Shubrook Bros. Creative
www.shubrookbros.com

With special thanks to Louise Grosart, Ruth Knowles, Natalie Barnes,
Ellie Farmer and Paul Terry

Bantam Books are published by
Random House Children's Books,
61-63 Uxbridge Road, London W5 5SA

www.rbooks.co.uk

www.kidsatrandomhouse.co.uk

Addresses for companies within The Random House Group Limited
can be found at:
www.randomhouse.co.uk/offices.htm

THE RANDOM HOUSE GROUP Limited Reg. No. 954009

A CIP catalogue record for this book is available from the British Library

Printed and bound by Sctoprint, Haddington

100%
THE WANTED

BANTAM BOOKS

Evie Parker

CONTENTS

THE WANTED 8
MAX 12
NATHAN 14
TOM 16
JAY 18
SIVA 20
POSTER 22
WHO'S YOUR MOST WANTED? 24
COULD YOU BE IN THE BAND? 26
POSTER 28
TUNED IN 30
MAX'S STYLE 34
NATHAN'S STYLE 35
TOM'S STYLE 36

SIVA'S STYLE..37

JAY'S STYLE 38

10 REASONS TO LOVE THE WANTED..39

POSTER...40

SEPARATED AT BIRTH?.......................42

LOVE WANTED...44

SAY WHAT?...46

FAN-DEMONIUM 48

STARS IN THEIR EYES 50

FAVOURITE THINGS............................52

EYE SPY!..54

WORD UP! 55

POSTER...56

TRIVIA...58

A-Z OF THE WANTED 60

THE WANTED

Calling all fans! Welcome to a full-on, fact-filled lowdown on the hot new pop sensation set to take the UK, and maybe even the world, by storm! Cool, cute and cheeky, these guys can pump out some seriously catchy tunes, bust some totally awesome moves and are guaranteed to get the dance floor jumpin'. Ladies, hold onto your hearts! Lads, hold on to your ladies, because this is the ultimate guide to the awesome new band on the verge of pop greatness – The Wanted.

5 FAST FACTS

1. The Wanted are signed to Geffen Records

2. They wrote approximately 50% of the songs on their first album

3. They share the same management company as The Saturdays

4. The guys went for an audition after they answered an advert in *The Stage*

5. They all live together in a bachelor pad in South London, which they admit is a bit messy! In fact, it's so messy that two cleaners have quit on the guys already! Can we apply for the job, please?

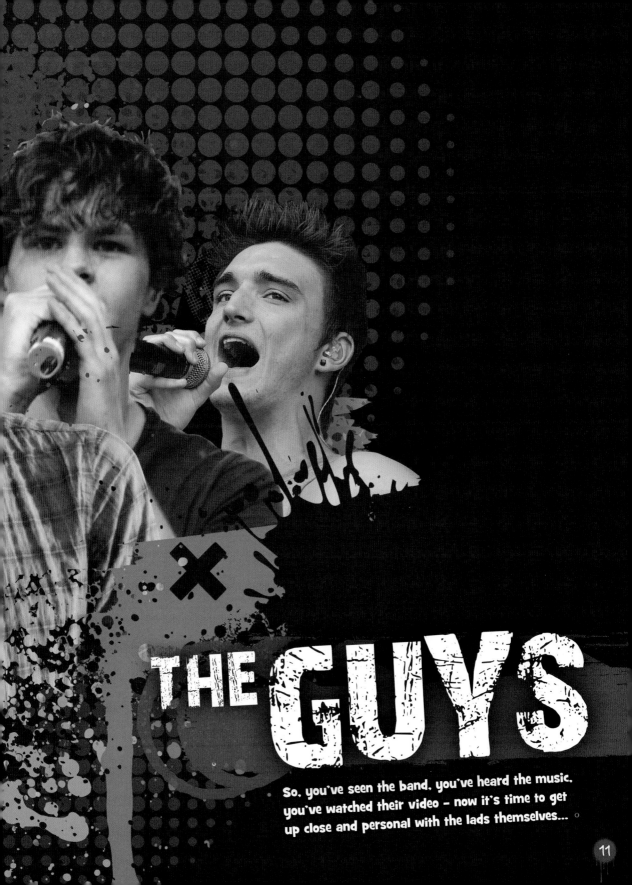

THE GUYS

So, you've seen the band, you've heard the music, you've watched their video – now it's time to get up close and personal with the lads themselves...

MAX

AKA THE HEART-THROB

Name
Maximillian Alberto Georg

Age
22

Date of birth
06/09/1988

Home town
Manchester

Height
5'8"

Eye colour
Grey

Hair colour
Dark brown

Max is definitely the party animal of the band. He's always up for a good time and loves a night on the town. Born in Manchester, his first love, and football team of choice, is Manchester City. Max originally had his sights set on a career in football and was pretty handy on the pitch! As a youngster he played professionally for Man City, and even made an appearance for his country as an England Schoolboy. Unfortunately for the sport (but not his admiring pop fans!) Max was forced to give up footie after suffering a bad hip injury. But he soon discovered music, and after a short stint in boy band Avenue (who you might remember being booted off *The X Factor*), he made it through the second sweep of auditions to secure his place in The Wanted.

DID YOU KNOW?

Avenue (Max's old band) were disqualified from *The X Factor* because they already had a management deal.

Max is always up for a good time!

LOVES

Steak – as rare as it can be!

HATES

Dry sponges! Apparently Fearne Cotton has the same phobia!

BEST BIT OF BEING IN A BOY BAND?

The girls!

He's super cute, with a super hot bod to match!

NATHAN

AKA **THE BABY**

Name
Nathan James Sykes

Age
17

Date of birth
18/04/93

Home town
Gloucester

Height
5ft '9ish

Eye colour
Green/blue

Hair colour
Brown

These lovely ladies trained at the same stage school as Nathan.

At seventeen. Nathan is the baby-faced youngster of the band. He knew he wanted to be a singer and performer from the age of six, started playing the piano at seven and has been in love with music ever since. As a super-talented lad he managed to win a scholarship to study at London's Sylvia Young Theatre School (Emma Bunton. Leona Lewis and Adele also went there!). Poor Nathan used to have to get up at 5 a.m. to make the three-hour trip from Gloucester to London to go to school – bet he's glad he did now! Not only the youngest. he's also the self-confessed quiet one. Apparently he's perfectly happy to sit back with a cup of tea and watch the other guys take on the action... ahhh. bless!

LOVES

Sitting at the piano and playing random songs.

BEST BIT OF BEING IN A BOY BAND?

Being on stage!

He's only young but he's got an amazing voice!

DID YOU KNOW?

Nathan plays the bagpipes!

HATES

Seeing Manchester United lose.

TOM

AKA THE CHEEKY ONE

Name
Tom Parker

Age
22

Date of birth
04/08/1988

Home town
Bolton

Height
5'10"

Eye colour
Hazel

Hair colour
Brown

Tom reckons he's up there with Max when it comes to partying! A self-confessed rocker and real live wire, it's not hard to believe that things get pretty hairy when he's around! When out celebrating their first single 'All Time Low' getting to number one, he accidentally set his T-shirt alight (don't try that at home, readers!). At sixteen, Tom started playing the guitar and has never looked back. He regards the guitar as his best friend and counts bands like Stereophonics and Oasis as major influences on his sound. According to the other members of the band, Tom is the messy one of the house – which must mean he's pretty untidy!

Tom, is that vest supposed to be see-through?

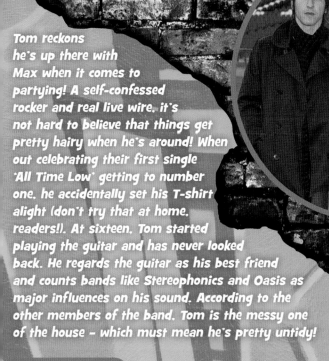

LOVES

All types of Italian food.

DID YOU KNOW?
Tom tried out for The X Factor but didn't get past the first round.

Tom loves the pop rock of Stereophonics!

BEST BIT OF BEING IN A BOY BAND?
The girls!

HATES
Not being able to get back to fans who've tweeted him.

JAY

AKA THE GEEK

Name
James McGuiness

Age
20

Date of birth
24/07/90

Home town
Nottingham

Height
6'1"

Eye colour
Blue

Hair colour
Brown

18

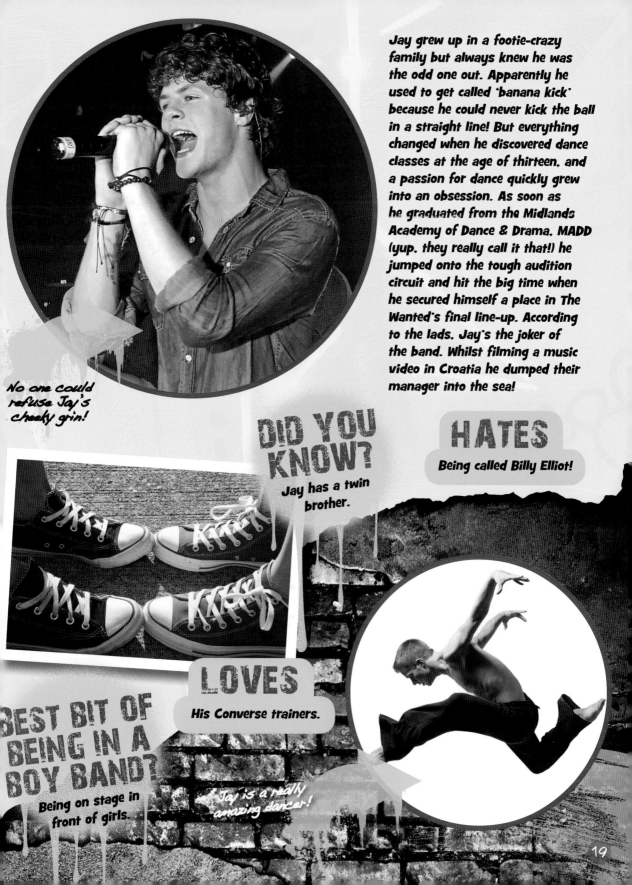

Jay grew up in a footie-crazy family but always knew he was the odd one out. Apparently he used to get called 'banana kick' because he could never kick the ball in a straight line! But everything changed when he discovered dance classes at the age of thirteen, and a passion for dance quickly grew into an obsession. As soon as he graduated from the Midlands Academy of Dance & Drama, MADD (yup, they really call it that!) he jumped onto the tough audition circuit and hit the big time when he secured himself a place in The Wanted's final line-up. According to the lads, Jay's the joker of the band. Whilst filming a music video in Croatia he dumped their manager into the sea!

No one could refuse Jay's cheeky grin!

DID YOU KNOW?

Jay has a twin brother.

HATES

Being called Billy Elliot!

LOVES

His Converse trainers.

BEST BIT OF BEING IN A BOY BAND?

Being on stage in front of girls.

Jay is a really amazing dancer!

19

SIVA

AKA THE ZEN ONE

Name
Siva Kaneswaran

Age
21

Date of birth
16/11/1988

Home town
Dublin

Height
6'1"

Eye colour
Brown

Hair colour
Black

With his smouldering good looks and a striking jaw line, it will come as no surprise that before Siva scored his place in The Wanted he used to be a model. In fact, the band's management company got in touch with his modelling agency to see if he'd done any singing – when it turned out that he had a stunning voice they were rather chuffed! But Siva's musical talents shouldn't be too surprising. He comes from a gifted family of eight kids, who he describes as Dublin's answer to the Jacksons! Siva's older sister nearly got into the final line-up of Girls Aloud and his twin brother, Kumar, also auditioned for the band but sadly didn't make the final cut.

Siva's sister nearly made it into Girls Aloud!

BEST BIT OF BEING IN A BOY BAND?

Getting Skittles from girls.

DID YOU KNOW?

Siva's trousers once fell down whilst The Wanted were performing on stage!

LOVES

Scented candles. He's allowed though, he's the zen one!

Just look at his perfect profile!

HATES

Leaving a cinema before the final credits.

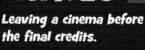
Popcorn

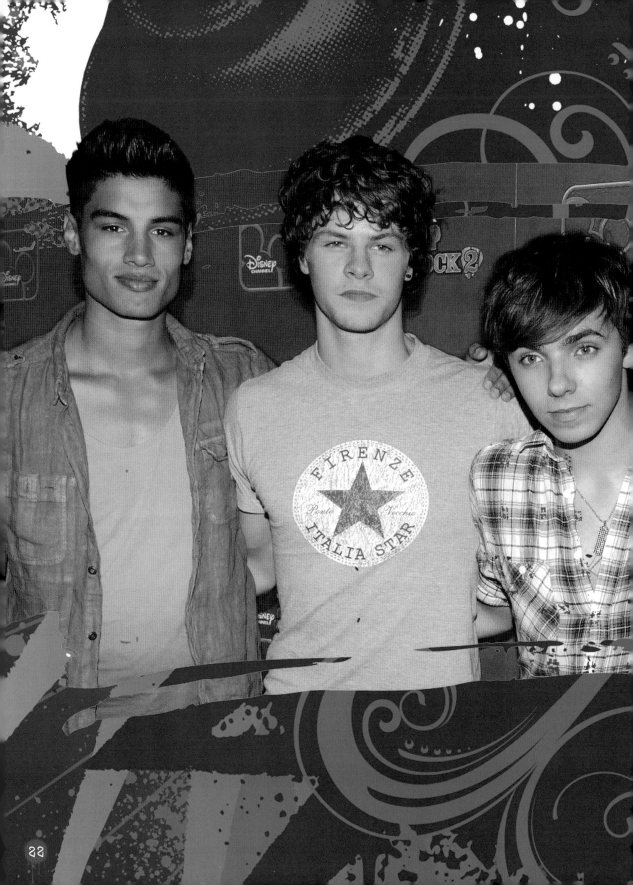

THE WANTED

WHO'S YOUR MOS⌐

Let's face it, girls would be happy to get their mitts on any one of the handsome fellas from The Wanted, but which one would be your perfect love match? Take a moment to answer the questions in this love-o-meter to work out who you should date and who'd be your mate.

1 It's Friday night and your best friend calls to tell you she's split up with her boyfriend. Do you:

A) Put on your best dress and party heels, race round and take her out for a wild night on the town?

B) Spend ages chatting to her, giving all your best advice?

C) Immediately start making a playlist of all your favourite calming tunes to help perk her up?

2 You're happiest when:

A) You're out dancing.

B) You're hanging out with your friends.

C) You're meditating with aromatherapy oils.

3 You're dancing away in your best party shoes when the heel breaks. Do you:

A) Carry on dancing?

B) Head home? It's getting late and you've had a great night anyway.

C) Slip on a pair of flip-flops you'd stashed in your bag? You're happiest dancing in flats!

4 You've lost your fave T-shirt. Do you:

A) Have a madcap five minutes running round the house before throwing on any old vest and heading out?

B) Ransack your bedroom then head over to your sister's to do the same because you know she'll have 'borrowed' it?

C) Calmly chuck on another one? You win some, you lose some. C'est la vie!

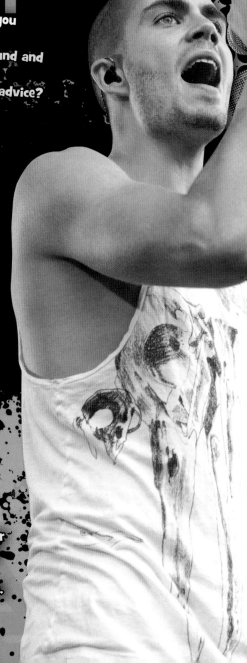

WANTED?

8 You like your music:
A) Cranked up to the max!
B) Hard edged and rocky!
C) Chilled out and relaxing.

5 Your horoscope tells you to have a quiet night in tonight. Do you:
A) Go out anyway? (You don't believe in that sort of stuff!)
B) Agonize over what to do then realize there's a pretty good film on TV so staying in seems like the best thing after all?
C) Stay in? You can't mess with fate!

+9 You suddenly remember your history homework's due tomorrow. you haven't started it and the house party of the century is happening at your friend's house! Do you:
A) Do it on the bus in the morning, as you could never miss this party?
B) Race to do the work and try to head over for a boogie later?
c) Light a few scented candles, then get down to studying?

6 You'd never leave the house without:
A) Your make-up.
B) Your phone.
C) Your *Little Book of Calm.*

x10 You're at school and you spot the boy you fancy walking down the corridor towards you. Do you:
A) Rush straight up to him? You've been dying to ask him out for ages and this is your BIG opportunity.
B) Give him a quick smile before heading over to your best mates for a morale boost and tips and advice on how to pluck up the courage to talk to him?
C) Take a moment to gather yourself. breathe in, then waltz over and calmly ask him on a date? You've been checking him out. he's been checking you out – some things are just meant to be!

7 Your eye make-up is:
A) Loud, bright and funky.
B) Pretty and breezy.
C) Nicely neutral.

IF YOU ANSWERED MOSTLY As
Wow! You are one smokin' party animal! Always the centre of attention and up for a laugh. you're the life and soul of the party. Your perfect love match would be either Tom or Max.

IF YOU ANSWERED MOSTLY Bs
Oh yes, you're one super-talented bod. Whether it's busting some amazing dance moves or writing some sweet music. your talents are limitless. Your perfect love match would be either Nathan or Jay.

IF YOU ANSWERED MOSTLY Cs
Blimey! You are one chilled-out soul. When times get tough or a bit crazy, you're the friend who is always relied upon to calm the situation down. If your bedroom is full of scented candles and soft furnishings then your perfect love match is Siva!

COULD YOU

Do you dream of super-stardom? Are you happiest being in charge, or do you have the skills but prefer not to be the centre of attention? Go with the flow and follow the questions to find out whether you could be in the band!

Your fave song comes on the radio. Do you:
A. Sing along at the top of your voice?
B. Hum along quietly?

Fashion and style is...
A. Everything!
B. There are more important things in life.

Your friend's taking a photo. Do you:
A. Fix your hair and take the prime spot in front of the camera?
B. Head for the back and hide?

Your biggest fear is:
A. Not wearing a matching outfit.
B. Making a fool of yourself.

What best describes you?
A. Fun and outrageous.
B. Smart and sensible.

You find yourself on stage. Do you:
A. Push to the front?
B. Focus on giving an amazing performance?

BE IN THE BAND?

Karaoke is:
A. 100% awesome!
B. Not for me!

A →

Complete this sentence:
Fame and fortune...
A. Is all I ever dream about.
B. Is a little bit overrated.

A →

IN THE BAND
You've got the confidence and charisma that'll take you to the top! So get set to work hard and prepare to take the world by storm!

B ↓

A ↗

B ↓

B ↗

You'd never leave the house without:
A. Your iPod.
B. Your diary.

Are you a:
A. Creative thinker?
B. Get up and do-er?

A →

BEHIND THE BAND
You love a good sing along, but you're happy not to lead! Your friends love that about you, which is why you're so popular!

B ↓

A →

In a crisis you are:
A. A calm and collected soul.
B. Panicky and all over the place.

A ↗

A ↑

WITH THE BAND
Although you're not openly seeking super-stardom, your quiet self-confidence and sense of style mean you definitely don't lack star quality!

A ↗

B ↓

Your friends would say you're:
A. A bit of a show off but lots of fun!
B. Modest and supportive.

B →

You hear a song. Do you:
A. Think, 'I would have done that differently'?
B. Dance?

B ↗

THE WANTED

TUNED IN

OK, it's clear The Wanted totally rock, but which bands rock their world? Their sound is an awesome urban blend of poppy tunes, edgy beats and with some indie riffs thrown in for good measure! Here's just some of the musical influences that are behind The Wanted.

NAME WANTED!

It was Nathan who came up with the band's name. They were in the studio working on their song 'Let's Get Ugly' – which samples a tune from classic Western film *The Good, The Bad and The Ugly* – when he had a vision of the guys on a 'wanted' poster! The lads thought it sounded pretty cool and it stuck! "It came out of the whole wild west vibe of that song, and just sounds cool, not too cheesy," adds Nathan. "We've got no time for cheese around here."

The boys have a tinge of Take That about them.

SOUNDS!

The guys may be a self-confessed lad-band rather than boyband, but their homage to some of the best British boybands is clear. Tom reckons, "We're a little bit of JLS, a bit of Take That and a bit of Westlife." But Nathan adds, "You won't find us sitting on stools in our suits and standing up for the key change!"

FAVOURITE BANDS

Tom – Oasis, Stereophonics
Max – Queen, Oasis
Jay – Coldplay, Damien Rice, Cat Stevens
Siva – John Legend
Nathan – Boyz II Men

Freddie Mercury of Queen

'90s boyband, Boyz II Men

The fit five are a pretty mixed bag when it comes to usical tastes, which is probably hat makes them such a fun and edgy combination. Tom agrees. There's something for everyone, he reckons. And Max would go further. 'We're like a buffet.' Erm, OK, Max!?

The Wanted: just like a buffet, apparently!

MUSICAL MIXES

Who would the lads love to collaborate with in the future?

Dizzee Rascal

Florence and the Machine

Justin Bieber – According to Siva, the guys are totally feeling the Bieber fever! Well, who isn't!?

Should JLS be worried?

The boys love Florence and the Machine.

Yes – The Wanted dig the Bieber too!

THE ALBUM – WHAT CAN YOU EXPECT?

Predominately upbeat, funky pop tunes. Expect some dirty baselines with a couple of acoustic, more piano-based songs thrown in too.

John Legend

The legendary songwriter, Cat Stevens

Chris Martin of Coldplay

Damien Rice

x

STYLE FILE

The Wanted are causing quite a stir on the pop circuit – not least because of their catchy dance tunes and hot bods – each member rocks their own unique style to match their personality. From combats to high tops, checked shirts to blazers, get the fashion lowdown on these urban lot who are smashing the clean-cut boyband mould with their edgy looks!

MAX

Max is the rough-and-ready member of the group. With his no-nonsense shaved head and facial stubble, his street style may seem effortless, but it takes time to look this good! He's a fan of the fuss-free vests, and with those guns, we're fans too!

Shaved head

Distressed denim jacket

Chest-baring T-shirt

Mustard, carrot-leg jeans (he loves these guys)

Converse trainers

NATHAN

With his super-cute face and sharp style, Nathan is the clean-cut member of the group. But he funks up his classic looks with an assortment of jewellery and battered trainers that give him a punk-chic appeal.

Floppy hair

Blazer

Necklaces

Bangles

Straight-legged jeans

Trainers

TOM

Spiky hair

This cheeky northerner rocks his favoured military/workman look. Distressed clothing has returned to the A-list's fashion radar, and with his baggy trousers and worn boots, he's got a sexy 'I just threw this on' kind of style. Tom's casual-cool vibe sometimes makes him look a bit like a plumber – a very fit plumber, mind!

Earring

Cut-collar T-shirt

Baggy joggers

Workman boots

SIVA

The model-turned-singer boasts an impressive quiff, ridiculously chiselled cheekbones and a slick dress sense to boot! Whoever said tie-dye belongs in the early '90s needs to check this combo out. Siva adds an urban twist to his tailored blazer with a pair of stylish workwear boots.

Big hair

Fitted blazer

Tie-dye T-shirt

Slim-fit trousers

Boots

JAY

Indie-kid Jay has a laid-back sense of style which matches his personality. He's usually decked out in a checked shirt or kaj T-shirt. which give him a low-key grunge look. Denim + flannel = lumberjack-chic á la Kurt Cobain. And we like it!

Curly locks

Checked shirt

Ripped, skinny jeans

White plimsolls

10 REASONS TO LOVE THE WANTED

It's not like we need to find any more reasons to love these feisty five, but just in case you need some persuading, here we go...

1 They are H.O.T. Full stop.

2 They have amazing vocals.

3 They are not your average cheesy boyband.

4 They love their fans and are appreciative of their support.

5 They're just average, down-to-earth guys from normal backgrounds.

6 They're musically talented. Nathan can play the piano (and the bagpipes!) and Siva and Tom can play the guitar.

7 They are all really good friends who live and work together.

8 They all have a great sense of humour and know how to party.

9 They write loads of their own songs.

10 Did we say they were hot???

39

THE WANTED

SEPARATED AT BIRTH?

Just in case you ever get tired of looking at these hotties, we've trawled the world of celebrity to find a whole host of other fitties that we think fit the bill for The Wanted lookalikes!

Jesse Metcalfe

Max

Zac Efron

Nathan

Taylor Lautner

Siva

Jay

James Beattie

Robert Pattinson

Tom

43

LOVE WANTED

We're at an all-time high when we look at these six-pack-tastic, drool-worthy lads. Whether you're into the shy and quiet type, funny and loud, or cool and collected, there's something for everyone in The Wanted. We've all got our favourite member – and that goes for the ladies in Celebville too. It looks like everyone wants to feel Wanted...

LEONA LEWIS

After her split with long-term boyfriend Lou Al-Chamaa, Leona didn't waste much time having fun with her newly single status. She took a liking to Max and gave him her number after they met at London club Whiskey Mist.

RIHANNA

The beautiful Barbadian met The Wanted at Capital FM's Summertime Ball. At the afterparty in Mahiki, Rihanna and Siva had a little dance and she's apparently sent him a couple of cheeky wee texts!

THE SATURDAYS

The Wanted boys have the same management as The Saturdays. and with five members in each group. it's little surprise to hear there's been some serious flirting – and even a football match. Tom. Max and Siva have said they'd like to date any of them! They're not picky!

At first I liked Frankie, because I knew who she was the most. But by the end of the tour, Vanessa was my favourite. She's got it all – she can sing. she can dance, she's hot!

Jay

HAYLEY WILLIAMS

Jay has a crush on the lead singer of American alternative rock band Paramore. He says she's got 'the perfect mouth.'

SINITTA

Max also has a soft spot for the older lady. He said. 'I saw Sinitta and she was hot. I love an older woman.'

KATE THORNTON

Nathan had a cheeky snog with older woman Kate Thornton when The Wanted were on *Loose Women*. He says she has an amazing smile and that he licked her teeth! Eurgh!

45

SAY WHAT?

Not only do these lads pump out some classic tunes, they're pretty hot on the interview circuit and have come out with some cracking lines! Here's just a selection of wise and wonderful insights from The Wanted!

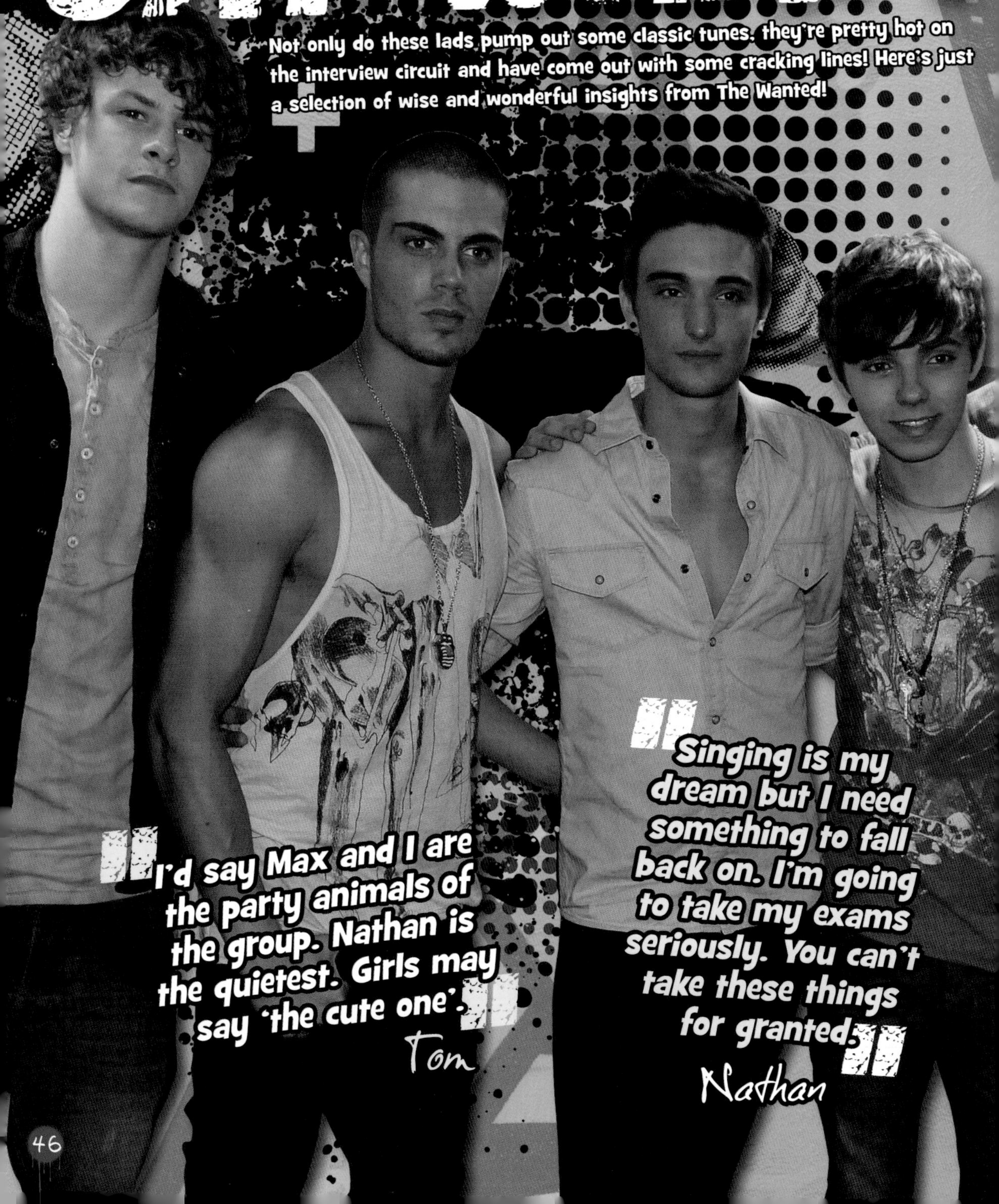

"I'd say Max and I are the party animals of the group. Nathan is the quietest. Girls may say 'the cute one'."

Tom

"Singing is my dream but I need something to fall back on. I'm going to take my exams seriously. You can't take these things for granted."

Nathan

"We're like a buffet."
Max

"We're all very different so hopefully people will like one of us! I'm really into my football and am a bit cheeky. Siva's pretty laid-back and really zen, Jay's a bit of an indie-kid and then Nathan – you think he's all young and cute but actually he's really dead dry and sarcastic. Oh yeah, and Tom – he's just a lad from Bolton."
Max

"I love clothes so it would be amazing to front a campaign for AllSaints."
Siva

"My guitar pretty much changed my life. I was never really into music before I picked it up when I was 16. Now it's like my best friend, wherever I am I just pick it up and start playing."
Tom

"I got a bit of stick when I was younger. I got called Billy Elliot so many times as I really liked dance while everyone else was into football."
Jay

"I slap on the moisturiser and sleep on silk sheets so I don't get wrinkles."
Siva

"It's awesome when the fans know your songs and sing them back at you."
Siva

"I love indie music, but I'm also not afraid to throw some crazy shapes."
Jay

47

FAN-DEMONIUM!

When it comes to their fans, The Wanted are certainly living up to their name. Before they had even released their first single, fans flocked to see the lads perform live around the country. Over 1,500 fans waited five hours for them at a London shopping centre, and it's become so crazy that their record label has hired former SAS soldiers to accompany them on their public appearances!

FAN FACT

Their video for 'All Time Low' has notched up over 2 million views.

FAN FACT

After performing at Old Trafford, the band spotted a group of fans stranded miles from home at 1 a.m. Max's dad gave the girls money to get a taxi home. Awww.

"It's hard to get used to them screaming at you. But it's nice too."
Max

FAN FACT

They are 'liked' by over 100,000 people on Facebook.

"We got off the plane and there were already girls in the airport screaming. It's so exciting to be here and we are still surprised by the reaction." *Jay*

FAMOUS FANS

Their speedy rise to fame has been supported by an array of celebs such as Alexandra Burke, Pixie Lott, Joe McElderry, The Saturdays, Tinie Tempah and Chipmunk.

"It's all about the fans. It's the least we can do." *Tom*

STARS IN THEIR

What better way to get close to your favourite band member than to check out his star sign?! Find out what makes him tick and then discover whether your destinies are aligned and if he could be your star-crossed lover!

MAX
STAR SIGN - VIRGO ♍

Virgo lads are super-trendy with a lot of soul. They're dependable and generally shy, but do have a hidden wild side! They're not massively romantic but once you've won a place in their heart they'll never let you out! Virgos always look for perfection, and can sometimes be a little bit fussy, but their charm and fun-loving personality mean you can never stay mad at them for long!

MAYBE BABY?
Are any of these celebs the perfect match for Max?
Megan Fox (Taurus)
Kate Bosworth (Capricorn)
Ashley Tisdale (Cancer)
Rachel McAdams (Scorpio)

Nathan ♈
STAR SIGN - ARIES

Arians are super-chatty! They're also pretty good-looking, although they never think it themselves. They have a huge love for life and are exciting to hang around with, and when they find the girl of their dreams they're prepared to pull out all the romantic stops to win her over. Because Arians know their own mind they can sometimes be argumentative but these lads are always up for chatting, so don't be afraid to give as good as you get!

MAYBE BABY?
Are any of these celebs the perfect match for Nathan?
Hayden Panettiere (Leo)
Vanessa Hudgens (Sagittarius)
Cheryl Cole (Gemini)
Mischa Barton (Aquarius)

EYES

TOM

STAR SIGN - LEO

Leo lads are big of heart and warm of spirit. They're playful and always up for a good time. They're massively faithful to their mates and girlfriends but if you ever cross a Leo, beware! They can be very feisty and are also very loyal.

MAYBE BABY?

Are any of these celebs the perfect match for Tom?
Reese Witherspoon (Aries)
Scarlett Johansson (Sagittarius)
Mary-Kate Olsen (Gemini)
Hilary Duff (Libra)

JAY

STAR SIGN - LEO

As well as having a warm heart, Leos are spontaneous and creative. They tend to have huge personalities – you definitely know when you've got a Leo in the room! Once they set their sights on something they usually get it!

MAYBE BABY?

Are any of these celebs the perfect match for Jay?
Kate Hudson (Aries)
Kelly Brook (Sagittarius)
Ashley Olsen (Gemini)
Ashlee Simpson (Libra)

MAYBE BABY?

Are any of these celebs the perfect match for Siva?
Nicole Scherzinger (Cancer)
Rihanna (Pisces)
Cameron Diaz (Virgo)
Gemma Arterton (Capricorn)

SIVA

STAR SIGN - SCORPIO

Scorpio guys are often dark and mysterious and a mass of contradictions. Because of this they're hugely adaptable to any situation and have a good sense of intuition. They are passionate, very intense and can be often be very strong-willed and stubborn, but Scorpios always have admirers!

51

FAVOURITE THIN

MAX

Football team:
Manchester City

Favourite animal:
Shark

Favourite TV show:
The X Factor

Favourite trainers:
Nike

Favourite food:
Steak

TOM

Football team:
Bolton Wanderers

Favourite animal:
Parrot

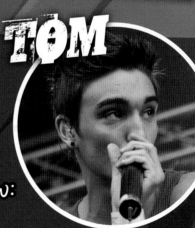

Favourite TV show:
The Inbetweeners

Favourite trainers:
Reebok

Favourite food:
Indian

OK, so The Wanted might be up there on the list with some of our top favourite things, but what makes these guys tick? Here's a whistle-stop tour through the bits and bobs that float their boats.

NATHAN

Football team:
Manchester United

Favourite trainers:
Converse

Favourite animal:
Cat

Favourite food:
Spaghetti Bolognese

Favourite TV show:
Britain's Got Talent

JAY

Football team:
Celtic

Favourite trainers:
Converse

Favourite animal:
Chimpanzee

Favourite food:
Pizza

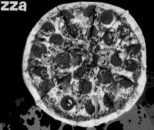

Favourite TV show:
David Attenborough nature shows

SIVA

Football team:
Manchester City & Bolton Wanderers

Favourite animal:
Dog

Favourite trainers:
Adidas

Favourite TV show:
Buffy the Vampire Slayer

Favourite food:
Shepherd's pie

EYE-SPY!

Take a close look at these two pictures of The Wanted and see if you can spot all 10 differences between them.

WORD UP!

Have a peek at the wordsearch below and see if you can find The Wanted-related words hidden inside it.

MAX TOM NATHAN SIVA
JAY THE WANTED GEFFEN
LADBAND FOOTBALL GUITAR

```
N A T H A T O M F I T
G M S I V H A N O X O
E C I B A E D F O K N
F X V L N W A N T E G
F N A T H A N X B L U
E A N D L N E M A X I
N M J X C T F N L F T
F S A F F E C G L B A
C F Y L A D B A N D R
```

Answers on page 61

THE WANTED

TRIVIA

Are you The Wanted's ultimate fan? Put your knowledge to the test with our tricky trivia to find out!

1 Which member of The Wanted had his sights on a career in football?
- A. Max
- B. Nathan
- C. Jay

2 Who is the youngest member of the band?
- A. Siva
- B. Tom
- C. Nathan

3 Who does not have a twin brother?
- A. Siva
- B. Jay
- C. Max

4 Which member of The Wanted says Oasis is one of their favourite bands?
- A. Nathan
- B. Tom
- C. Jay

58

5 What was Siva's occupation before he joined The Wanted?
- [ ] A. Actor
- [ ] B. Model
- [ ] C. Jockey

6 Which star sign is Jay?
- [ ] A. Gemini
- [ ] B. Aries
- [ ] C. Leo

7 What is Nathan's favourite TV show?
- [ ] A. Britain's Got Talent
- [ ] B. The X Factor
- [ ] C. Star Trek

8 What was Max scared of doing when The Wanted performed at the Capital FM Summertime Ball?
- [ ] A. Forgetting the words
- [ ] B. Tripping on stage
- [ ] C. Dribbling

9 When is Tom's birthday?
- [ ] A. 4th May 1987
- [ ] B. 4th August 1988
- [ ] C. 4th December 1989

10 What film was the inspiration for The Wanted's name?
- [ ] A. The Good, the Bad and the Ugly
- [ ] B. Billy the Kid
- [ ] C. Most Wanted

Answers on page 61

A-Z OF THE WANTED

OMG – even the alphabet is after a piece of The Wanted!

Max met Simon Cowell when he was in his former boyband!

The Wanted in all their glory!

Tom totally digs Oasis.

A	**'All Time Low'** – Their amazing debut single!
B	**Bagpipes** – Nathan can actually play these!
C	**Carrot-leg jeans** – We'd never heard of them till Max started wearing 'em!
D	**Dance** – There are no stools for this active bunch!
E	**Earring** – Tom rocks one, and we likey!
F	**Football** – They talk about it... a lot.
G	**Geffen Records** – The Wanted's record label.
H	**Hot** – Oh yes, ladies, this is one band full of sweet eye-candy!
I	**Internet** – These guys keep in touch with their fans by Tweeting all over the shop!
J	**Jay** – He's got a pair of dancing feet, just don't call him Billy Elliot, OK?
K	**Kiss** – Yes please!
L	**Lad-band** – These chaps are a self-confessed lad-band. Boys need not apply!
M	**Max** – He's a lovable rogue.
N	**Nathan** – He's the fresh-faced cutie.
O	**Oasis** – Tom's favourite band.
P	**Piano** – Nathan can also play this instrument.
Q	**Quintuple** – It's a handsome fivesome!
R	**Rihanna** – She gave her number to Siva!
S	**Siva** – He's smouldering and sultry, with a jaw line to die for!
T	**Tom** – He's one awesome guitar player!
U	**Urban style** – Clean-cut won't make the grade with these lads, it's street all the way!
V	**Vests** – They're back in fashion thanks to these guys!
W	**Wanted poster** – The inspiration for their name.
X	**The X Factor** – Where we first saw Max in boyband Avenue.
Y	**Youngest** – At 17, Nathan's the baby of the band.
Z	**Zen** – Thank goodness Siva's there to keep the others in check!

ANSWERS

PAGE 54   EYE-SPY!

PAGE 55   WORD UP!

```
N A T H A T O M F I T
G M S I V H A N O X O
E C I B A E D F O K N
F X V L N W A N T E G
F N A T H A N X B L U
E A N D L N E M A X I
N M J X C T F N L F T
F S A F F E C G L B A
C F V L A D B A N D R
```

PAGE 58-59

TRIVIA

1 - A	6 - C
2 - C	7 - A
3 - C	8 - C
4 - B	9 - B
5 - B	10 - A